Ravenscourt
B·O·O·K·S

The Mountain Is On Fire!

By

Carole H. Gerber

SRA

Columbus, OH • Chicago, IL • Redmond, WA

The **McGraw·Hill** Companies

Photos: Cover, ©Art Wolfe/Image Bank/Getty Images; **11,** ©David Muench/Corbis; **15,** ©James A. Sugar/Corbis; **24,** ©Michael T. Sedam/Corbis.

Illustrations: Paul Montgomery

SRAonline.com

 SRA

Send all inquiries to:
SRA/McGraw-Hill
8787 Orion Place
Columbus, OH 43240-4027

Printed in the United States of America.

ISBN 0-07-601582-3

  2 3 4 5 6 7 8 9 MAL 08 07 06 05 04

1 ❖ **The Volcano** 1

2 ❖ **The Red Cloud**..........................6

3 ❖ **Mount St. Helens Erupts** 10

4 ❖ **Some Stayed Behind** 17

5 ❖ **Why Mountains Blow Their Tops**..................20

6 ❖ **Warnings Save Lives** 25

—Chapter 1—

The Volcano

The dark cloud seemed to be stuck to the top of the mountain. Mother said it looked like a pine tree. I saw the tree too. To me, the smaller clouds were its branches. The cloud looked like it was full of dirt and ash.

Because we lived far from the mountains, we couldn't tell which mountain it was. My uncle wanted to see it up close. He wanted me to go too. But I told him that I had to finish my lessons.

The year was A.D. 79. *I did not go to a school. My mother could not read, and my father was dead. My uncle could read and write. So, he became my teacher. He was the commander of a fleet of ships.

I loved my uncle. I knew he was proud of me. We had the same name. His name was Pliny. I was called Pliny the Younger.

On the day we saw the dark cloud, my uncle got a letter. It was from a woman who lived in Pompeii. Pompeii was at the foot of Mount Vesuvius. The woman was afraid that the mountain* would erupt. She wanted my uncle to save her.

My uncle took his fleet into the bay and headed for Pompeii. Mother and I watched him sail off. He did not seem afraid. But we were afraid for him.

We looked out over the water. We saw rocks and fire blow out of the mountain. Ash fell from the sky. Still my uncle's fleet sailed on to save people. Mother started to cry.

The sky grew dark. We could no longer see my uncle's ship. I finished my lesson. Mother made dinner. Later we went to bed.

The next morning the ground started to shake. Mother ran into my room. "Come outside, Pliny!" she shouted. "It will be safer there!"

I ran outside.

—Chapter 2—

The Red Cloud

*A man came to help us. He said we were in danger. He told us to leave as quickly as we could. Buildings were falling all around us. Our house was still all right, but not for long.

We knew we had to leave. We could see the huge cloud. It was full of flames.

The red cloud came closer to land. It was coming right at us!

Fine dust and ash fell from the sky. Mother started to cough. She could not breathe. She told me to leave her. "I will die happy," she said, "if I know I* did not cause your death."

I would not leave my mother. I took her hand, and we sat down. Soon the air became black and still. We heard people crying. Some were yelling for help.

Suddenly we saw a river of fire coming toward us. It flowed down from the top of the mountain. I knew it would kill us if we stayed.

Mother and I sat there for a long time. We did not talk. We held hands. We waited for the end to come.

But then the cloud lifted, and we could see the sun. Our house was still there. We were alive, but 2,000 people had been killed.

My uncle died near his ship. The thick dust and gas had stopped his breathing.

Pompeii had been a large town. Now it is a ruin. No one lives there. The town was buried under ash.

—Chapter 3—

Mount St. Helens Erupts

Fast forward to spring 1980. Think of another mountain. The place is Washington State. The mountain is Mount St. Helens.

It was spring, and the mountain was beautiful. There were lots of flowers and birds. The water in the lakes and streams was deep blue.

But the ground was shaking! Steam was rising from the quiet mountain. Scientists knew this was a bad sign.

*In March there had been quakes. At first there were just a few. Then there were 2,000 more!

Some small eruptions had blown holes in the side of the mountain—more bad signs. By early April most of the area had been closed.

Only a few scientists were allowed to be there. People who lived in the area were told to leave. They were supposed to be allowed back on May 17 and 18 to get things from their homes.

The mountain was alive and not for the first time. Mount St. Helens had blown its top four other times.* And there had been many little eruptions.

Long ago, American Indians called Mount St. Helens the "smoking mountain" and "fire mountain." They did not have machines then to warn them of an eruption. They watched the sky. They felt the ground. They could not stop the volcano. They could only watch.

In 1980 scientists had machines to warn them. But their machines could not stop the volcano.

On the morning of May 18, Mount St. Helens blew its top. Mud and lava shot from the top. Rock and ash flew. The sky turned black.

The first blast lasted for nine hours. It was like a big bomb. The heat in the cloud was 500°F.

Every living thing within ten miles of Mount St. Helens—people, animals, birds, and fish—died. For miles and miles, trees were gone. And all this took place in the first five minutes of the blast!

The eruption blasted rock, snow, ice, and lava down rivers and valleys. It swept away cars, buildings, trees, roads, and bridges.

The blasts kept coming. After three days, one side of the mountain was gone. And 57 people had died.

Wind carried the ash a long way. People all over the world found ash from the Mount St. Helens eruption.

—Chapter 4—

Some Stayed Behind

On May 18th Dan Miller went to take pictures of Mount St. Helens. It was part of his job.

Dan was far from the mountain that morning. Even so, he felt the danger. He said, "I saw a big, angry, black cloud rising up."[1]

Dan knew he was not safe. He got in his car. He left as fast as he could.

People were told to leave the area. But some would not go.

*David Johnston was one of them. He worked near Mount St. Helens. His job was to watch the mountain.

David knew he could be killed, so why did he stay? He wanted to make sure other people were safe.

He saw the first bits of fire and ash shoot up. He made a call. His last words were, "This is it!"

There were others who would not leave. One of them was 83-year-old Harry Truman. He lived at the foot of the mountain. He loved living there. He also loved his 16 cats.

Harry knew the volcano could* kill him. He watched others leave. Still he would not go.

His wife was buried nearby. Maybe the idea of leaving was worse than dying. Maybe Harry wanted his life to end near the things he loved. We will never know for sure. A landslide buried Harry and his cats.

[1]Used with permission from TIME For Kids magazine.

—Chapter 5—

Why Mountains Blow Their Tops

Only some mountains can blow their tops. The cone shape of these mountains is a sign. It shows you they are volcanoes.

Volcanoes are filled with water, gas, ash, and rock. The rock turns to liquid. Why? There is too much heat and pressure.

The liquid rock is called *magma.* Part of the magma swells and rises. Then it takes up too much space inside the mountain. The magma has to find a way out.

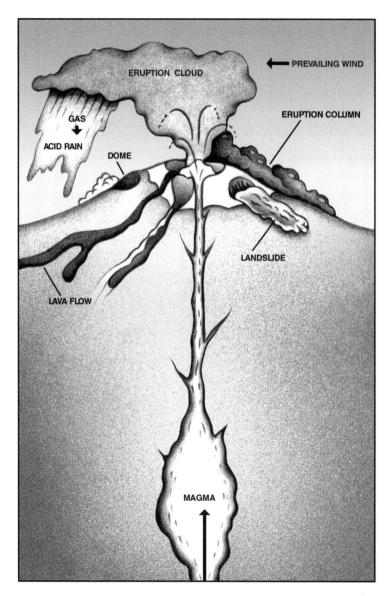

21

*Hot gas leaks first. It might leak for years or for a short time.

If there is still too much pressure, the mountain breaks open. Boom! The volcano blows its top.

Where does the pressure come from? It comes from deep inside Earth.

There are huge pieces of solid rock deep in the earth. Earth's center is so hot that it makes the rock move. Magma moves in between the rocks. The pressure builds.

If there is too much pressure, the volcano can erupt. Magma, gas, ash, and rock shoot out.

Air makes the magma, now called *lava,* thicker. Hot* lava flows out of the volcano. It kills everything in its path.

Over time, lava helps make the soil rich. After Mount St. Helens erupted, the land looked as bare and gray as the moon. But within a year things started to grow again. Little green plants shot up from the ash.

Today small trees grow everywhere. Flowers dot the land. Insects, birds, and animals once again live on the mountain.

Will the mountain stay quiet? No one knows for sure. If it does, in a hundred years the land will look much like it did before the blast.

—Chapter 6—

Warnings Save Lives

Did you know there are 540 active volcanoes in the world? Around 15 to 20 volcanoes erupt every day.

Scientists gather facts to find out what volcanoes will do. What they find out helps save lives.

In A.D. 79, no one in Pompeii knew that Mount Vesuvius would erupt. When it did, 2,000 people died. They had no time to get away.

*In 1980 when Mount St. Helens erupted, 57 people died. The warnings gave many people time to leave and saved many lives.

How do scientists know when to warn people? Small quakes are one sign of danger. They are too small to be felt by people. Machines keep track of these quakes.

Cracks in the earth are another sign. Big cracks are a sign there is a lot of pressure inside the volcano. This means the volcano could erupt soon.

Scientists also keep track of how much gas leaks from the cracks. A volcano leaks a lot of gas before* it erupts.

Since 1980 Mount St. Helens has erupted 22 times. Most of the eruptions have been small. But scientists keep track of the mountain. They read the signs. Then they can warn people to leave if it again becomes a mountain on fire.